STEPHIE MORGAN

THE BLOG STARTUP

The Complete Guide on Being a Blogger, Discover All the Useful Information You Need on Starting Your Own Blog Today

Descrierea CIP a Bibliotecii Naționale a României
STEPHIE MORGAN
THE BLOG STARTUP. The Complete Guide on Being a
Blogger, Discover All the Useful Information You Need on
Starting Your Own Blog Today / Stephie Morgan. – Bucharest:
Editura My Ebook, 2020
ISBN 978-606-983-601-9

STEPHIE MORGAN

THE BLOG STARTUP

The Complete Guide on Being a Blogger, Discover All the Useful Information You Need on Starting Your Own Blog Today

My Ebook Publishing House
Bucharest, 2020

TABLE OF CONTENT

INTRODUCTORY

Have you heard other people talking on and on about their "blogs" while all you could do was smile and nod?

Yes, "blog" is a peculiar word, conjuring visions of mosquito-infested swamps, and you can't imagine why people would be eager to get more visitors to theirs.

But eager they are. In spite of the rather unfortunate name, blogs are the hottest things in communication since cell phones. Blogs are websites on which almost anybody can post information on almost any topic as often as they like.

Blogs can be devoted to a single factual topic, or they can be the equivalent of personal diaries in which people record their private thoughts and observations about the world. The contents of a blog are limited only by the imagination of the blog's creator, or "author".

If you find the thought of your own blog appealing, and have an Internet- connected computer, here are some suggestions to help you both get a blog going and build an audience with whom you can share it:

First, choose a topic for your blog on which you will enjoy communicating, and prepare your material. Your opinions on a subject are fine, as long as they are based on some underlying. There are always going to be those who know as much, about a topic as you, and if you want a credible blog, you need to be able to back up your statements.

Add some humor and personal experiences to your topic if you can. Writing a travel blog about places you have actually been, and about colorful locals whom you actually encountered, will make much better reading than just posting facts and figures picked up from travel sites and TV shows.

Offer material which will appeal to both novice travelers – like how to avoid pickpockets – and more seasoned ones – like the best undiscovered attractions in a specific destination.

Don't limit your blog to your own experiences. Keep it updated with news that might affect those interested in your subject. While your experiences can give people valuable insight, recognize that your opinions about what happened to you or about a specific product are, after all, just opinions. Give people factual information which they can weigh for themselves.

Keep you blog current. On the Internet, news can become old in a matter of hours, and what happened a month ago is ancient history. Telling people considering a trip to Thailand that Thailand experienced a coup last September will do nothing to help them decide about a trip next month.

Updating them on the peaceful state of affairs in Thailand today, however, will.

Updating your blog will require a commitment from you. You'll need to establish a regular time to search for and write about fresh news, and get it posted. There'll be times when not much has happened, and there'll be times when you can't type fast enough. But two or three times a week are not too many to post something new.

Even if it's only to tell your readers that not much has been going on, share a few thoughts, and tell your readers when to next check in for your next entry, make an appearance. Your audience will keep coming back as long as they know you are.

Keep you blog as simple as you can, without sounding like you don't have a complete grasp of your subject. You want to appeal to as many people as possible, and nothing will drive those newly interested in a subject away faster than lots of technical jargon and statistics. You can provide complex information, as long as you make the effort to put it in user-friendly terms.

Find a memorable name for your blog, and use your blog editing feature to post it in large, bold-face type. "My Hiking Blog" will probably sound interesting only to Mom and Dad and only because you never write or call them while you're out adventuring. "Climbing through the Clouds" will appeal to those who either tackle the high places of the Earth, or want to.

Every so often, say, at the end of each month, archive your existing blog posts. Your blog editor will let you do this in a less than a minute. The entries will still be available for new blog readers who want to catch up, or those who want to reference your earlier writings. And list keywords for your archived work so that new traffic will be able to find its way to you.

Finally, make sure your blog is professionally presented. You have a spell checker, so use it.

Proof-read your copy and correct any grammar or punctuation errors before you post your work. If you're not sure whether you are using a word properly, get help from an online dictionary. Respect your readers as intelligent, well-informed people who could just as easily spend their time elsewhere.

These suggestions may make your entry into the world of blogging more successful, but it's up to you to commit to building and keeping an audience.

CHAPTER 1

BEGINNERS GUIDE TO BLOGGING

A blog is basically an online journal wherein you can digitally pen down your thoughts, ideas, opinions and practically anything that you want people to read.

Blogs come in different styles, formats, and settings, depending on the preference of the user. Many blogging sites, offer built in features such as hyperlink, straight texts, pictures etc. Some blogging sites, even allow you to put video and mp3's on your blogs.

Instead of writing texts, some bloggers choose to make their blogs more audio friendly, by using spoken word entries. This is called audio blogging.

Basically, a blog contains these features:

- Title - which allows you to label your post.

- Body - this is the content of your post.

- Trackback - other sites can be linked back to your blog.

- Permanent link - every article that you write has a URL.

- Comments - this allow readers to post comments on your blog.

One of the advantages of blogging, is that it is made of only a few templates. Unlike, other websites that is made up of numerous individual pages. This make it easier for blog users to create new pages, because it already has a fix setting that include: slots for title, body of the post, category, etc.

This is especially useful for first time users, since they can start blogging right away. They can choose from a number of templates that blogging websites provide.

Anyone who wants to start a blog can do so by becoming a member of a blogging website of their choice. Once they've become members, they automatically become a part of that particular blogging community. They can browse through other bloggers pages, and link them back to their own blogs. They can also make comments on other members' blogs.

Blogging is not just limited to personal usage. There are a lot of blogs that follow a theme such as: sports, politics, philosophy, social commentary, etc. These blogs espouse on their specific themes. This way blogging becomes a medium in which people can share their knowledge and opinions about a variety of themes and topics.

Some bloggers even use their blogs as a means to advertise. Some authors advertise their books on their blogs. While other bloggers, use their blogs to shed light to currents issues, events, news and catastrophes.

Nowadays in education, blogs also play an important part. Professors use blogging to document the lessons that they have discussed and taught. This way, students who have missed classes, can easily catch up with their assignments.

A lot of entrepreneurs benefit from blogging by promoting their businesses on their blogs, with millions and millions of people logging onto the net every day, blogging has become a lucrative move. Some bloggers who run online businesses promote their merchandise online. While others profit through advertisement.

But by far, the most popular blog type is the one that takes the form of a personal journal. This is the kind that is usually used by first time bloggers. Individuals who want to document the daily struggle of their everyday lives, poems, rants, opinions, find that blogging offers them a medium in which to express themselves.

Bloggers usually communicate within themselves. This is one of the appeals of blogging. It creates a community of people sharing their ideas, thoughts, and comments with each other.

Blogs varying in topics, themes, and set-ups, can be found in blog directories. First time users who want to get an idea of what the blogging world is all about can browse through a number of blogs using these directories. This way they'd get an idea of what these blogging communities are like.

Blogging is popular all over the world. Blog is short for the term weblog. There are no rules when it comes to blogging. Bloggers have the freedom to express themselves however way they want, and the best thing about blogging, is that most blogging sites are free.

There are numerous blogging websites to choose from in the net. This give first time users the option of joining a blogging community that appeals to their interests.

Just search any blogging directory and you'd get a listing of a lot of blogging sites that are available on the net. It's easy to search a blogging directory, because it is organized according to category. This way you would get exactly what you are after. Blogging is really for everyone. It is fun, simple and easy.

CHAPTER 2

BLOGGING FOR MONEY

Blogging has become one of the most powerful economic forces on the Internet today. Thousands of speedy hands have taken to entering content into blog fields as a way to earn income or write about their life experiences.

From its early beginnings with sites like LiveJournal, blogging for money has become the latest craze. Today, the more popular blogs like jossip.com and Perezhilton generate close to a million dollars each year worth of advertising revenue. Blogging for money can certainly yield this result with tremendous work!

Webmasters can make extra money blogging through advertising programs, sponsorships, affiliate programs, merchandising, AdSense, and more.

Advertising options for those making money through blogs have been skyrocketing over the past year with the most popular method through contextual ad programs like AdSense that pay-per-click.

With targeted ads that reflect your blogs content, consumers are more apt to click. Create a blog with higher paying "keyword ads" ($1.00 a click is common!) and lots of traffic and an extra thousand can be made every month!

Discovering income from home blogs also means signing up for affiliate programs. Programs like Commission Junction, Amazon, and ClickBank pair you up with companies who pay commissions for sales through your blogs' banner ad leads. These products may include soaps, clothing, computer products, and more. All bloggers have complete control over the type of ads appearing on their sites. A third way to make money online blogging is through sponsorships.

Highly regarded blogs with thousands of visitors every month can be acclaimed by companies looking to sponsor the blog for advertising space. Although it takes hard work to reach the top, money making opportunities are endless. Remember, there is more room at the top than there is at the bottom!

Finally, making money through blogs may mean creating other digital assets to sale to act as secondary income streams.

Your blog may complement an e-book or course you're selling and may double up as a discussion board to retain clients. In addition, bloggers can advertise freely on their sites.

Monetizing blogs can happen in many different ways.

Many freelance writers find themselves hired by bloggers to come up with dynamic content for their journals. This content serves as sales pitches to the contextual ads that may appear on the site, benefiting both the blogger and the "hired gun."

To start blogging for money, type in blog into any Google search. If you want blogs to pay you instead of launching your own operation, you can do that too. Blogging is an excellent way to earn that side cash.

CHAPTER 3

AFFILIATE MARKETING AND BLOGGING

Affiliate marketing is one way in which bloggers utilize their blog to generate revenue.

The amount of revenue generated by a blog featuring affiliate marketing links may vary significantly depending on the amount of traffic the blog receives as well as the compensation offered for the affiliate marketing. Affiliate marketing essentially entails creating a link on the blog to another company's website.

The other company then compensates the blog owner according to a previously agreed upon contract. This compensation may be awarded in a number of different ways. The blog owner may be compensated each time the advertisement is served, each time a unique website visitor clicks through the advertisement or each time a blog visitor performs a desired action such as making a purchase or registering with the website.

This article will discuss some aspects of affiliate marketing which bloggers should understand including selecting opportunities carefully, maximizing the income potential for these opportunities and understanding the requirements associated with these affiliate marketing opportunities.

Selecting Affiliate Marketing Opportunities

There is a wide variety of affiliate marketing opportunities available. Many different companies and websites offer affiliate marketing opportunities. In most cases the blog owner simply needs to submit the website address of his blog along with some other basic information for approval. In most cases the company is not likely to reject the application unless the content of the website is deemed to be objectionable or otherwise in conflict of interest with the company's goals.

However, although getting approved to display affiliate links on your website is a rather simple process, this does not mean blog owners should select these affiliate marketing opportunities without discretion. It is a far better idea to carefully select affiliate marketing opportunities with companies who are of interest to the target audience of the blog.

A well-focused blog that is reaching a specific target audience should seek to display marketing links directing website traffic to companies which complement the blog without acting as direct competition to the blog. This helps to ensure the blog visitors will not only be interested in the affiliate marketing links and therefore more likely to click on the links but will also help to ensure the blog visitors do not find the affiliate marketing links to be bothersome.

Maximizing Affiliate Marketing Opportunities

Once blog owners have selected affiliate marketing opportunities it is time to consider how they can maximize the profit generated by these links. There are a couple of critical factors which blog owners should carefully consider to help maximize their profit from affiliate marketing. This includes regularly evaluating the effectiveness of the affiliate links and promoting the blog to maximize traffic.

Blog owners who incorporate affiliate marketing into their blog should regularly evaluate the effectiveness of the affiliate links. This can be done by comparing the percentage of blog visitors who click on the affiliate links to the overall blog traffic.

A blog which has high traffic but a relatively small percentage of visitors who click on the affiliate links should consider making changes to attempt to entice more blog visitors to click on the links. These changes can involve the aesthetics, size or location of the advertisements. Making only one change at a time is recommended because it makes it easier for the blog owner to evaluate which changes are most beneficial.

Blog owners can also help to maximize the profit from their affiliate marketing opportunities by doing self-promotion to drive additional website to the blog. This will likely be beneficial because higher website traffic will generally translate to greater profit from affiliate marketing.

Additionally, the blog owner may want to occasionally mention companies for which they are an affiliate to generate interest in the advertisements on the website.

Understanding Affiliate Marketing Requirements

Finally, blog owners should pay careful attention to the affiliate marketing agreements they enter. This is important because some companies may place restrictions on the usage of a link to their website. This may include restrictions such as avoiding objectionable content, not including links or advertisements for direct competitors or restrictions on the appearance of the affiliate links.

Failure to adhere to these guidelines may result in the blog losing affiliate privileges and the blog owner being denied compensation.

CHAPTER 4

EFFECTIVE BLOGGING

Perhaps "blogging" isn't such a graceful word. For me, personally, it sounds like a worded drudgery the way cereals can be soggy, skies can be foggy, and the way minds can be groggy.

But for now, it's too late to rename this shortened word for web-logging. Widespread blogging is nevertheless one of the most engaging Internet developments of the past few years. As a medium it gives rise to many new and worthy voices and plays a new and vital force in shaping opinions, political realities, trends, and even our language.

I believe that a blog is simply a tool to use for someone who's got something to say. Let me be clear in saying that a blog is a poor choice for someone who needs a megaphone to scream out to cyberspace in order to elicit a meaningful response from Internet users.

If you want attention and want it now and expect blogging to bring it to you, then this will surely be a disappointment. However, if you like to write and engage others on subjects of which you have some command or experience, then it's a wonderful application with which you can interact with people who share similar interests as you. The hype is well founded.

Anyway, here's a list of blogging tips…

1.) Be Topical:

Cohesiveness in message is not optional. Readers may or may not be interested in your topic, but if your message is haphazard that few will bother remembering to return to your blog because it essentially would offer nothing to remember.

This doesn't mean blogs can't jump from subject to subject. For instance, a blog with a humorous focus has all the leeway in the world for subject matter, but it would be foolish for such a blog to turn the humor on and off. In such an example, the aspect of humor would be content's glue, the strength of the blog. The beauty of staying on point and on topic is that eventually, due to the nature of the Internet, you will find those interested solely in your topic. (as opposed to online diaries. There are millions of them on the internet, few have any readers.

Email me with examples if I'm wrong and I'll be able to show you why you're howing me a blog and not a diary.)

2.) Refresh Your Content:

Create a schedule and stick to it. Realizing that blogging requires time and effort, don't create unrealistic expectations and be unable to deliver. An occasional lapse or holiday is generally understood but readers returning to find stale, outdated content are going to find another blog with similar content. New blogs and RSS feeds are popping up on a daily basis. If you have worked hard to develop an audience and a community you don't want to lose them due to lack of communication.

And remember, what's old is not new and, for blogs, thusly not interesting.

2006 isn't the time to rail against Enron or Vanilla Ice. Insight doesn't matter much to yesterday's news.

3.) Clear Language Counts:

Blessed is the blog with a clear line of logic. Write without inside jokes, clique-y catchphrases or ambiguous logic. First time readers need to be close to your message. They are more likely to return to blogs that strike them positively. If the first read is confusing there will not be a second read.

4.) Feed the Spiders:

Search engines take notice of active blogs and blog search engines are especially sensitive to activity. If nothing else, search engines are smarter today than they were yesterday and are only getting smarter. In constantly improving they are seeking to aggregate quality; quality blogs are updated several times a week, if not daily, as opposed to once or twice a month. I don't mean to scare you but a big spider is watching, so dance for them.

5.) RSS:

Think of RSS like a magic to blogging world, because that's the effect it's had. RSS feeds are a way to exponentially sound your voice to the interested. These feeds are a great means to increase the distribution and readership of your original content.

6.) Spell Check:

Hey man, use the spell-check. I do – if I didn't you probably wouldn't have made it to #6. It only takes a minute and can save you from looking like a hack.

Your weblog audiences will be small at first. And, frankly, that's the way it should be. Who are you to think that half the internet will flock to you after three or four posts of your blog, anyway?

If you tough it out while maintaining quality, readership will materialize. You will link to good, relevant blogs and, in turn, they will to you. While your voice may be unique, your niche likely isn't and if your content is emitted smartly to the Internet those relevant readers will respond through readership and interaction.

CHAPTER 5

COMMON BLOGGING MISTAKES

It happens so often it's almost like clockwork. Business blogs are started with high hopes and then disillusion sets in when the results aren't what they hoped for.

A lot of it has to do with these simple but common mistakes.

Not Asking For Comments

Bloggers always agonize over the lack of comments. But the problem is not that people don't read the blog or don't want to comment but the blogger hasn't given the opportunity for readers to comment. Just like asking for people to order a product, you've got to coax people to spend their 3 or 4 precious minutes to comment on your blog. Ask for opinions. People love giving it.

Ask for reader's experiences, input or help to accomplish something. Ask people to suggest something to you e.g. You're getting incorporated, ask people for suggestions, tips and recommendations. Asking also tells people you're open to suggestions and alternative views, further improving the image people may have of you.

Not Hosting On Their Own Domain

Give thought into your blog. Don't just jump on the bandwagon. You need to figure out where it's taking you before you hop on for the ride. Like any web site you may build, think of your blog as a long-term marketing communication channel. A BlogSpot or TypePad URL is not only unprofessional, you don't own it. Nothing against these blogging services; they're excellent tools but for long term marketing purposes, go for your own domain.

This way you control where you want to publish the blog to. Tomorrow, if you outgrow these services, you can easily export your blog to another tool, another host without losing too much established traffic. A domain is also easier for people to remember and easier for you to publicize.

Not Maximizing Their Blog Content

Many businesses quit blogging because they feel it's too much work. True, like everything else, you gotta work on a blog but you don't have to break your back over it. Sometimes you may have a paragraph here and there about a topic that just isn't big enough for an article.

You know what? You're going to have many more of these impromptu thoughts and ideas – publish it to your blog. Later, you can come back and gather these paragraphs, compile them into a complete article or even a book.

That's only one way of maximizing your work. Have you written articles in the past? How about e-courses, audio transcripts or books that aren't in publication anymore? Recycle. Break them up and post them on your blog. In fact, if you have lots of this type of content, you can even get your assistant to post them for you.

Publishing Too Often

I know what you're thinking. This sounds like complete the opposite of everything you've ever learnt about blogging. Truth is, the blogging world changes. What works yesterday may not today. This is one of them. There are countless blogs already jostling with you for your reader's time. More are being started by the day.

Who has the time to read so many blogs? It's come to a point people are forced to cherry pick the blogs they read. Even when they do read yours, you're not safe yet. If they can't keep up with your blogging pace, they'll drop you no matter how good your information is. Keep a balance.

Feed information to your readers not dump a truckload on them. Every market is different. Some can tolerate higher number of posts a week, some can't. You should know your market and test accordingly.

Falling For Short Term Methods

Ah, this is my favorite. If you can have a favorite pet peeve that is. Every week, you hear about people dishing out the newest, coolest blogging tactic, best blogging tool that's sure to sky rocket your business to success or bull doze your way to the top search engine listings. Consider how any offer will help you advance your business two, five or ten years from now. Is it really in line with your marketing direction? If it isn't drop it. It also helps a lot if you can have a reliable source whom you can consult and help put things into perspective for you.

One of the most powerful qualities of a blog has nothing to do with search engines, tagging or pinging. These things do have a place, but they aren't as powerful as the relationship opportunities between you and your customers.

Although these mistakes are common, they are also very easily rectified and don't cost much money. All of these suggestions are born out of my own trial and error and they've worked out nicely. Try it yourself.

CHAPTER 6

ESSENTIAL BLOGGING TOOLS

You finally decided to take the blog leap. You've heard all about the marketing and search benefits so you stepped up to the plate and signed up for a TypePad, MovableType or WordPress blog software package and now you're a blogger.

Okay, now what? Add the ten essential blogging tools listed below and you will also be well on your way to creating and promoting a blog that is a powerful marketing tool. I'll explain the use of the tool and offer some suggestions.

Feed Reader

The best way to learn about blogs and blogging is to read, or at least scan, lots of blogs. One of the wonders of blogs is that you can have every new post from every blog you want to read delivered to your desktop or to online location via RSS, so you can easily read and scan the posts of many blogs in a very short time. Newsgator is a good online choice for feed reading and also has a version that integrates with Outlook. I use a free online service know as Bloglines. http://www.bloglines.com

Subscriber Center

You need to make it easy for your blog visitors to subscribe to your blog's RSS feed – so they can read your blog in their favorite feed reader. The best way to do this is to go to FeedBurner and burn your own RSS feed their and use the tools they provide to set up automatic subscriber links so people who want to use Bloglines, Google Reader, MyYahoo or Pluck, for instance, can click on one button to subscribe. Tech types can figure this out without the buttons but why not make it easy for anyone to figure out.

Side note – subscribe to each of these yourself and you will force some blog spiders to visit your site. http://www.feedburner.com

Email Subscription Option

A lot of people will never get the whole feed thing, but everyone gets email. Create an option for people to subscribe by giving you their email address – they will simply receive your blog posts like an email message. FeedBurner offers this service for free. FeedBlitz is another option or, if you already have an autoresponder email list service they may offer this service. AWeber offers this and helps me integrate these blog email subscribers into my other mailing lists.

Blog and RSS Directories

There are hundreds of blog and RSS directories and getting listed in many can be a good thing. I use a piece of software called RSS Submit, but you can also visit Robin Goode's frequently updated list and submit your blog and feed by hand.

Hint: subscribe to the RSS feed he offers and you will be notified when new directories are added.

Ping Service

Pinging is a term used for letting the various blog and RSS directories know when you have posted new content. Again, FeedBurner offers this as an automatic option called PingShot and you should activate it. PingGoat and Ping O Matic are other options but they require that you visit and update your record each time you post new content.

Bookmark Manager

As you surf around the web or hop from blog to blog you may find sites that you want to point out to your readers. Online bookmark managers allow you to bookmark and categorize web and blog pages as you collect them and are a great tool for managing all of the stuff you find on the web.

Blog Stats

I like to track a few key stats in real time because it shows what other blogs might be linking to you or posting about your blog. A lot of people just like to track this kind of thing for fun and frequently visit sites like Technorati. I like to track it for networking opportunities.

I use a tool called MyBlogLog because it allows me to see where traffic is coming from but also tracks what links on my blog visitors are clicking on. It's amazing how this data can help you write more effectively. (MyBlogLog also ranks your links so visitors can see which links on your site are the most popular.)

Desktop Posting

With most blog software you must go online and post using a set of tools provided by the blog software. Many bloggers like to use a desktop application to create and submit their posts as it gives them some extra tools and allows them to more easily integrate content and files on their computer.

Tell a Friend Script

My blog software (pMachine) has a feature that allows a reader to click a link and send the post to a friend. This tactic brings me lots of readers.

Republish Your Feed Headlines

The ability to republish your blog posts on other web pages, sites you own or sites of strategic partners is a great way to expose folks to you blog content. One more time we turn to FeedBurner for a painless way to republish your blog post to any web page you choose with something they call BuzzBoost.

Printed by Libri Plureos GmbH in Hamburg, Germany